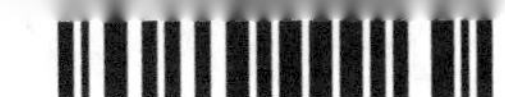
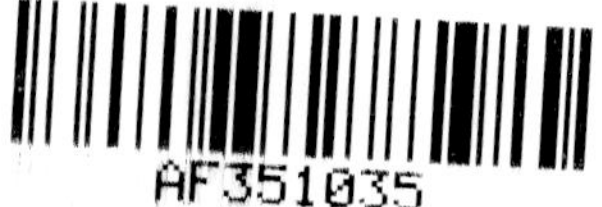

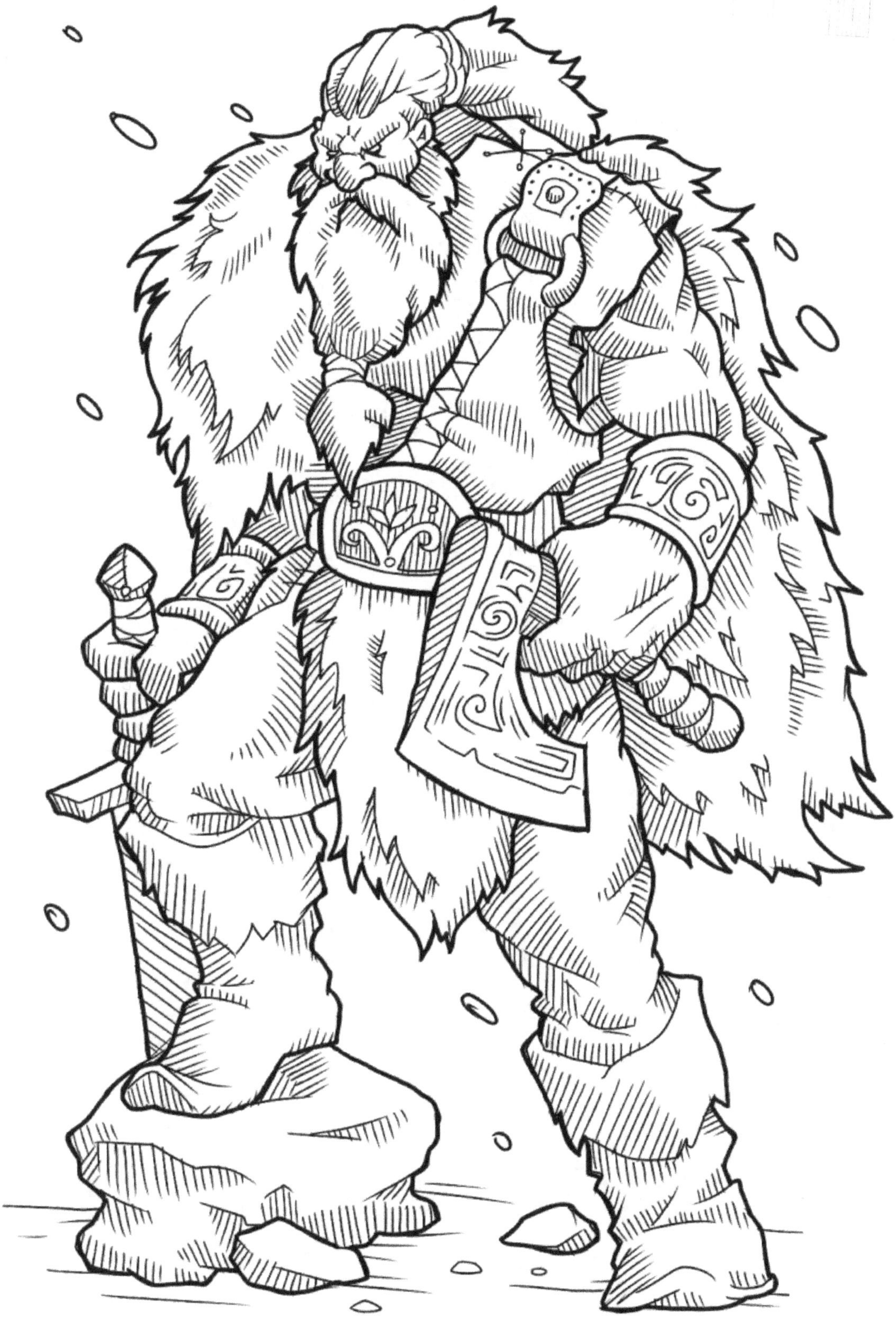

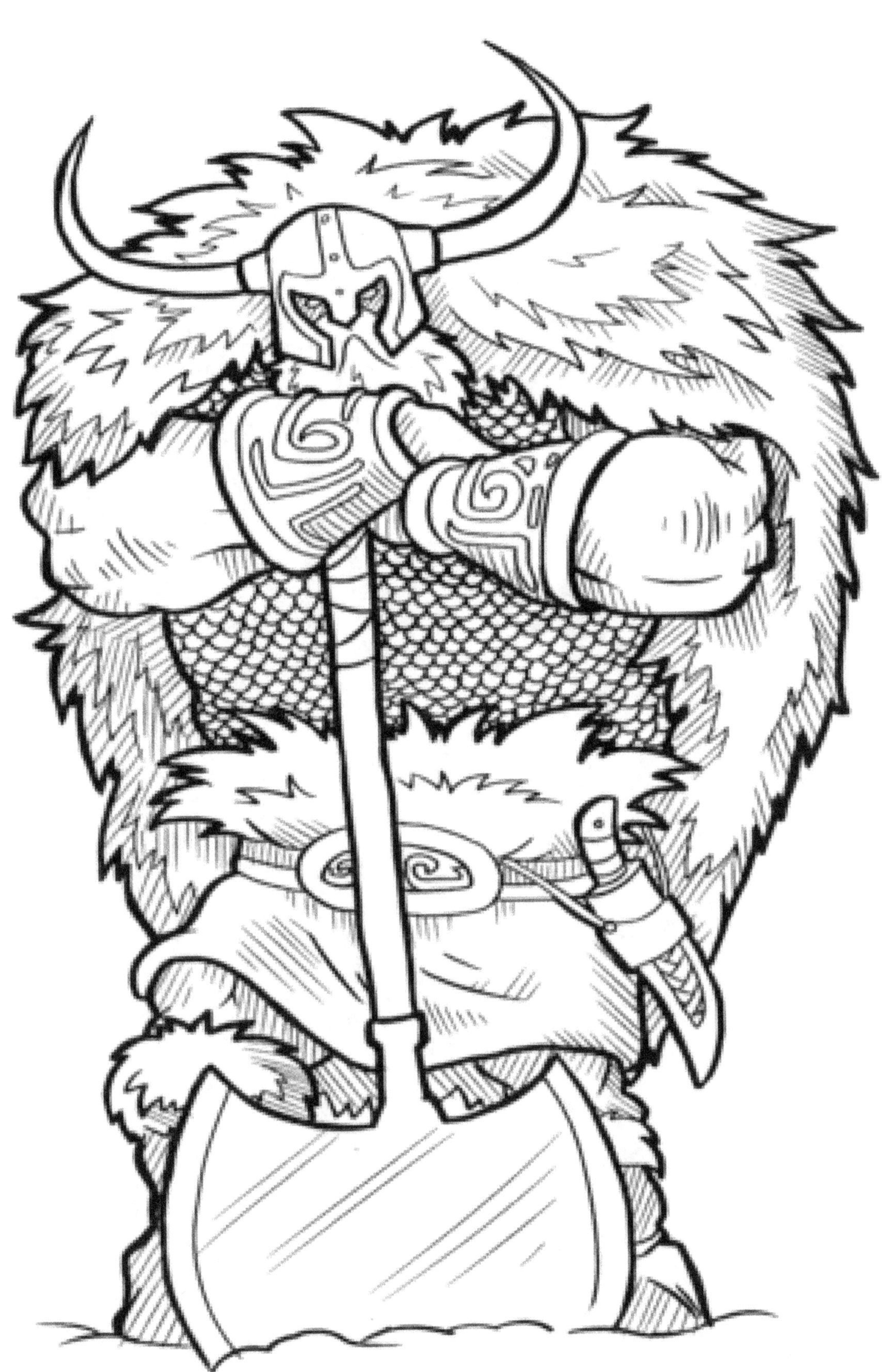

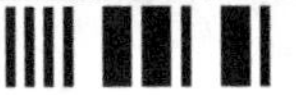

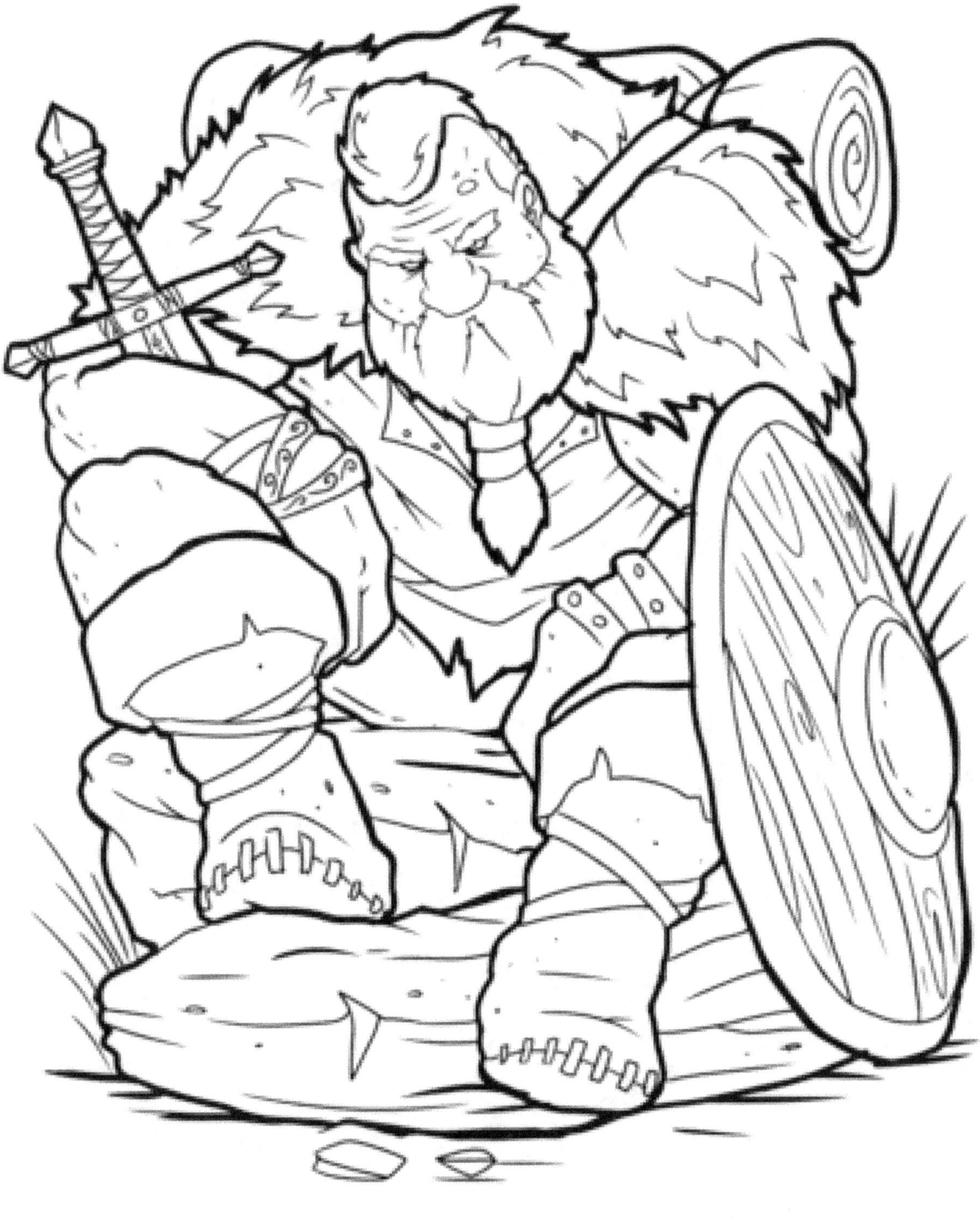

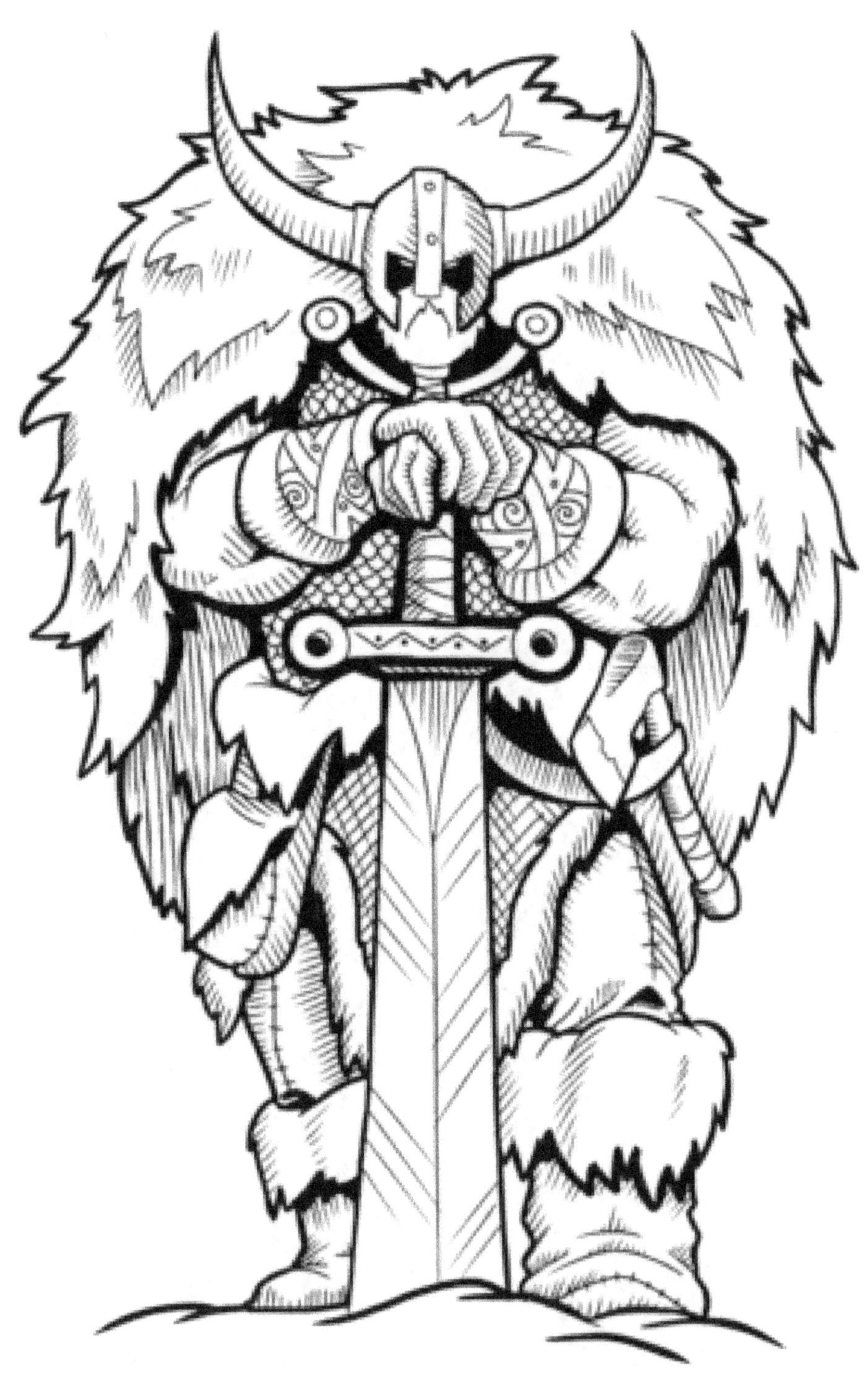

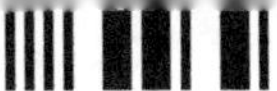

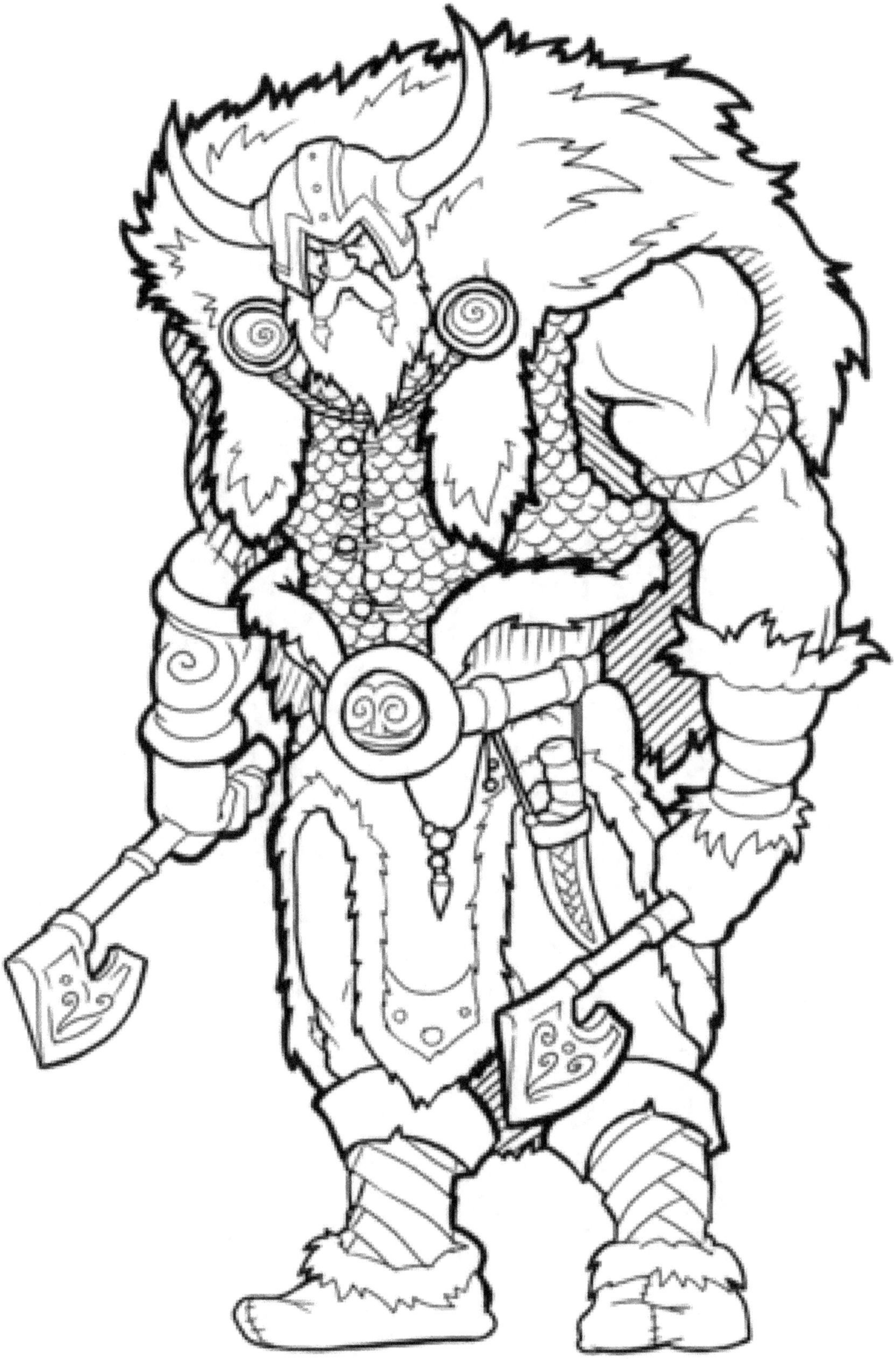

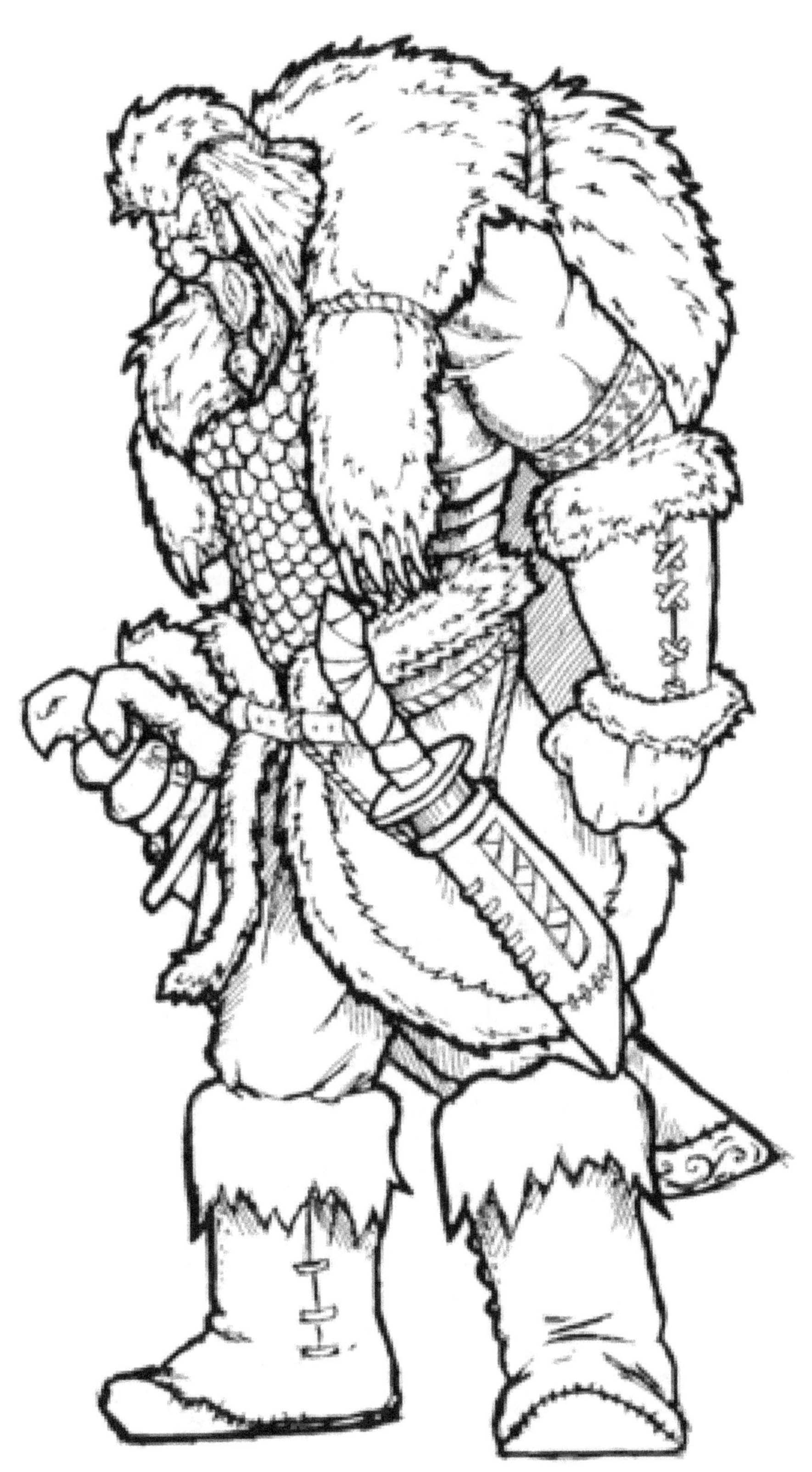

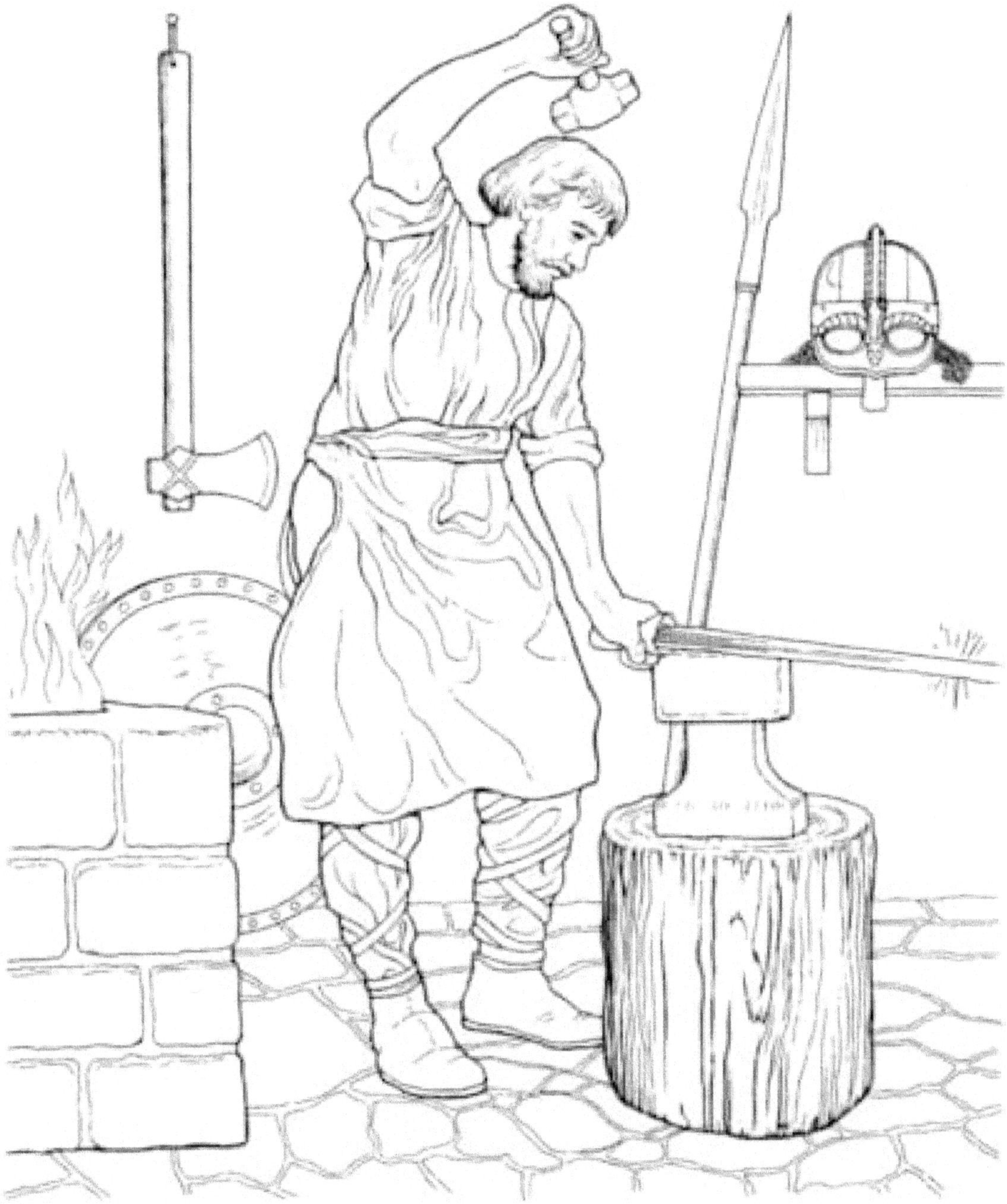

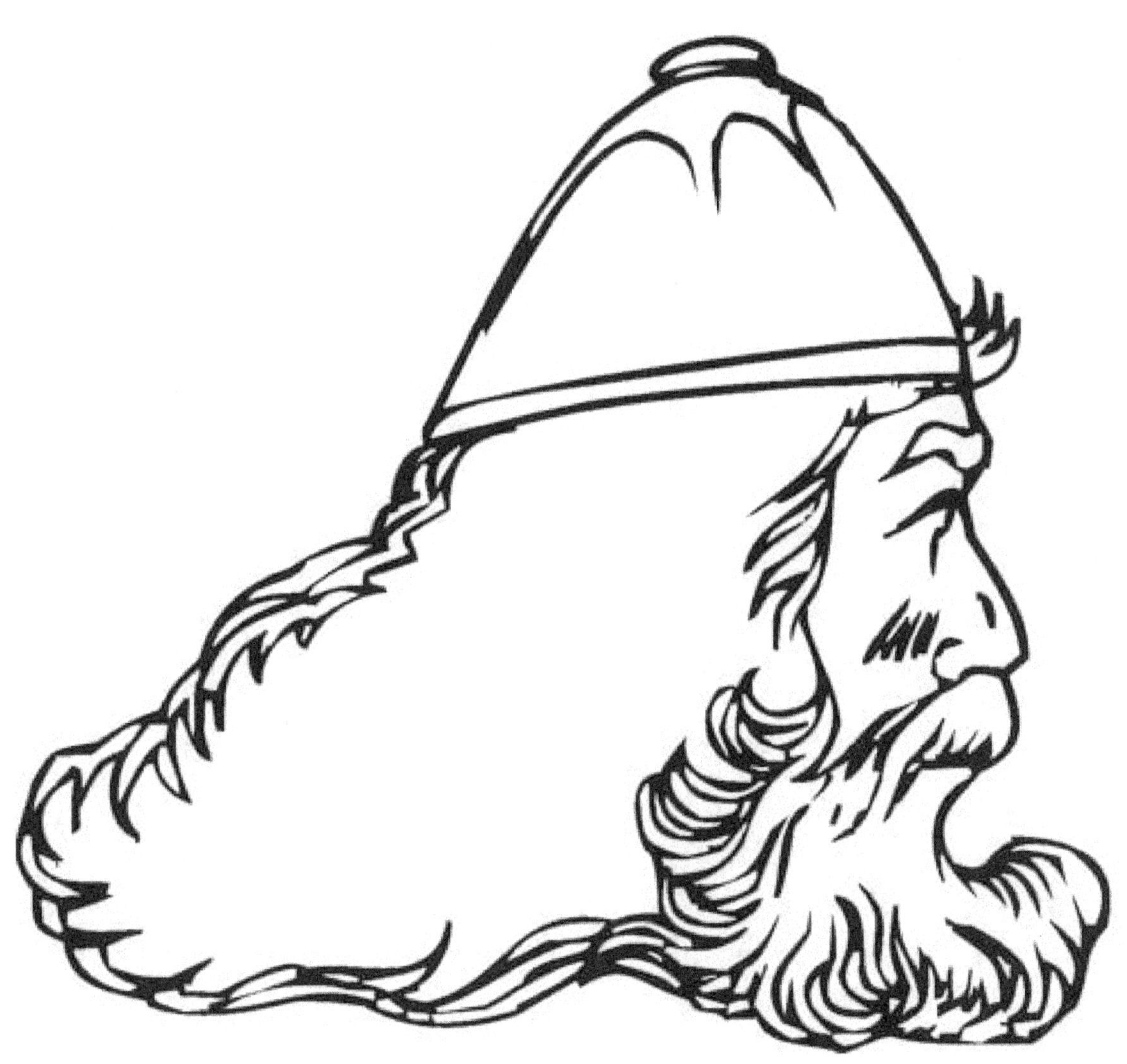

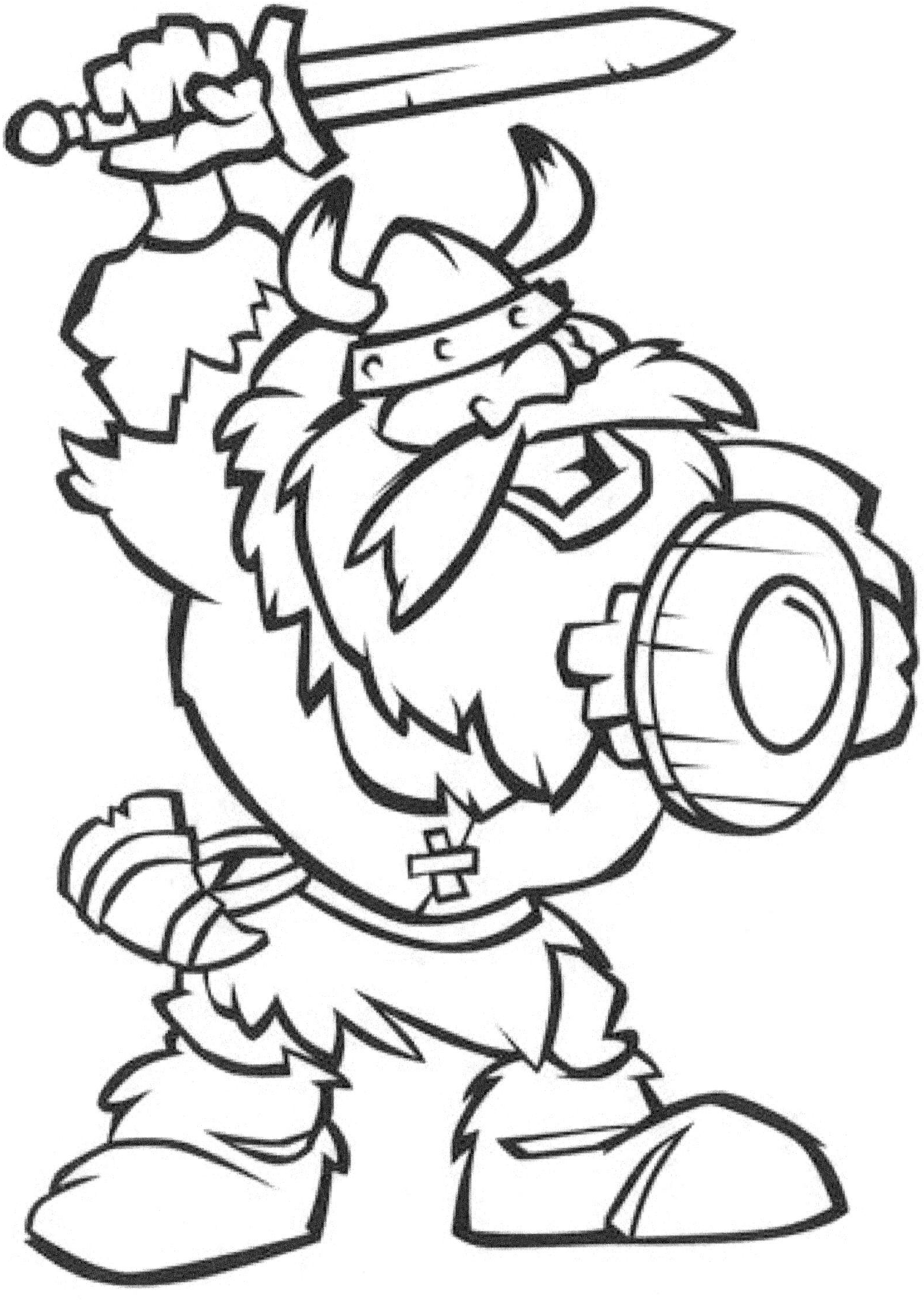

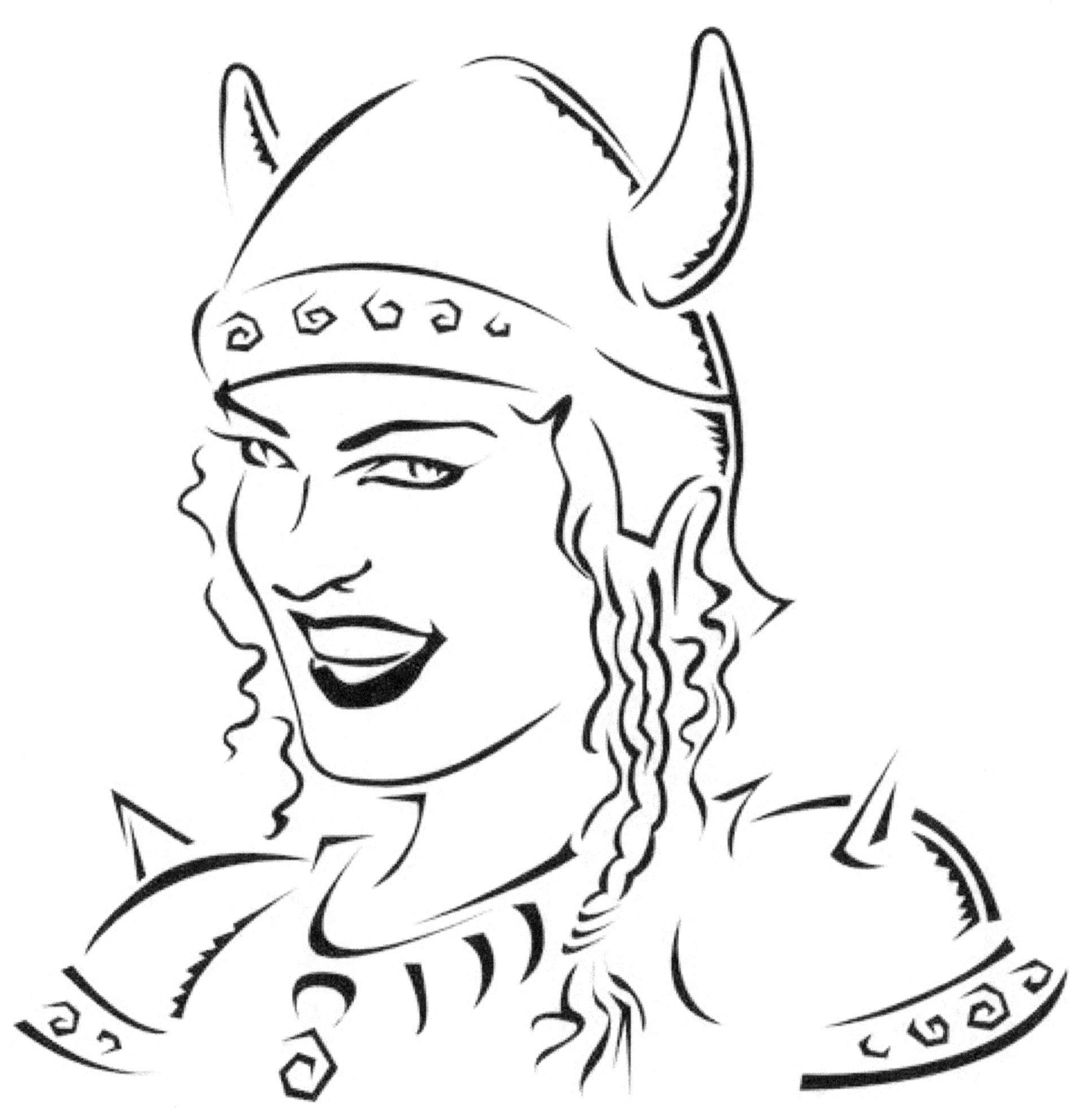

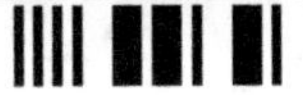

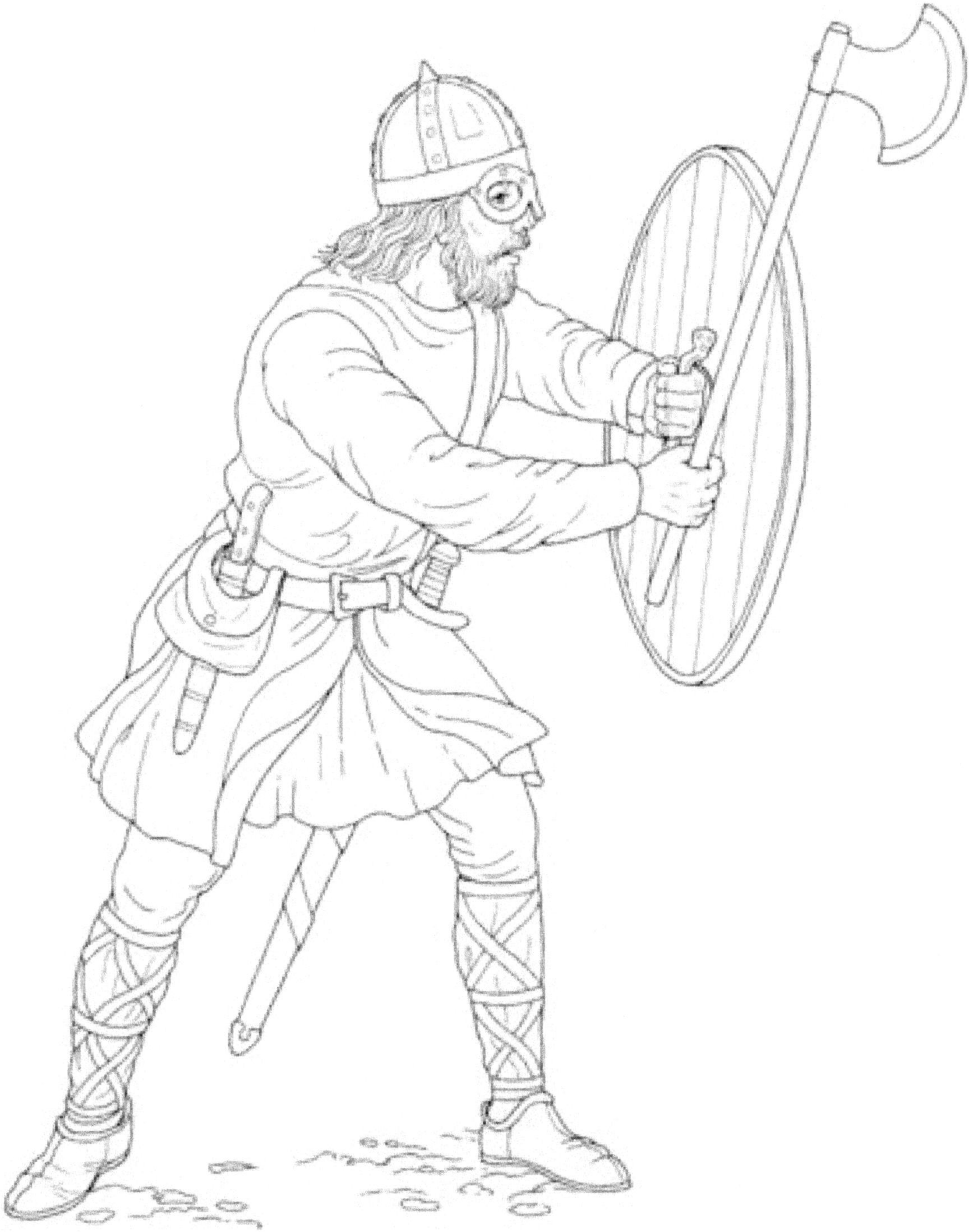

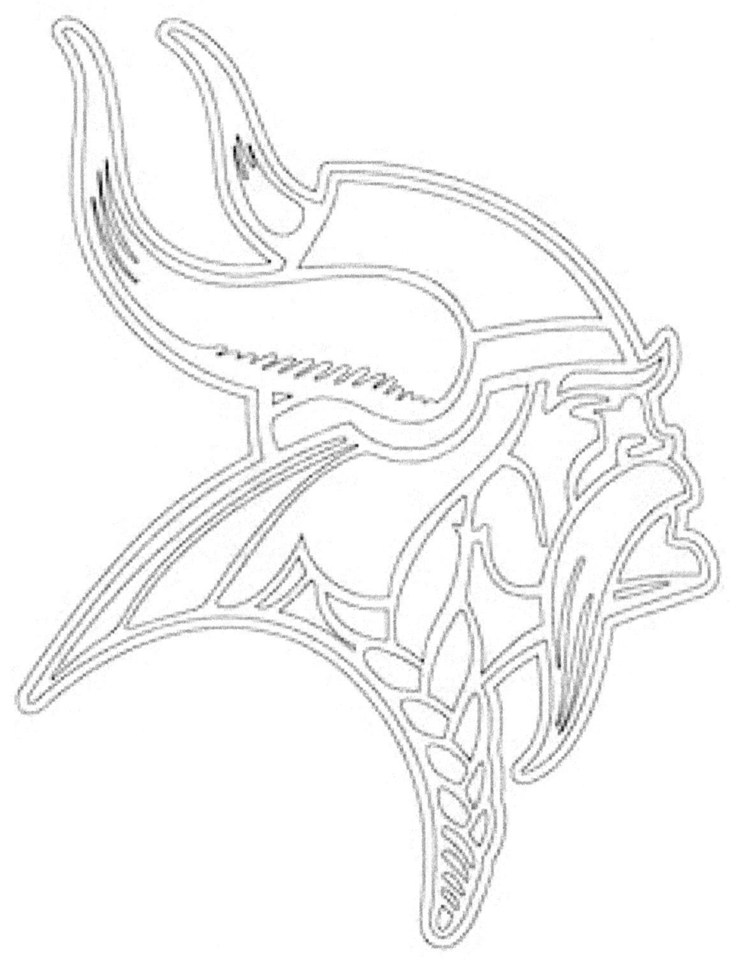

VIKINGS

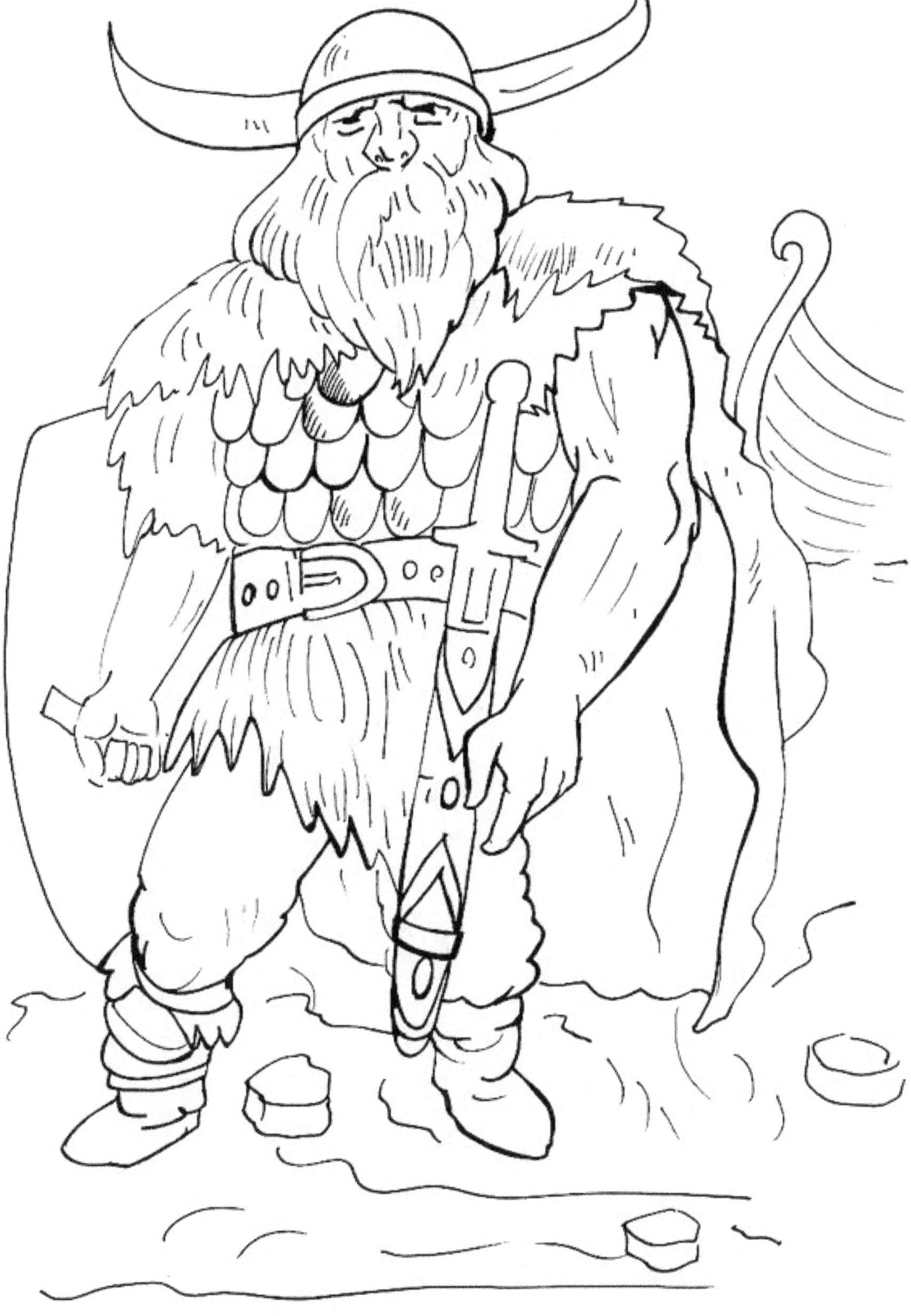

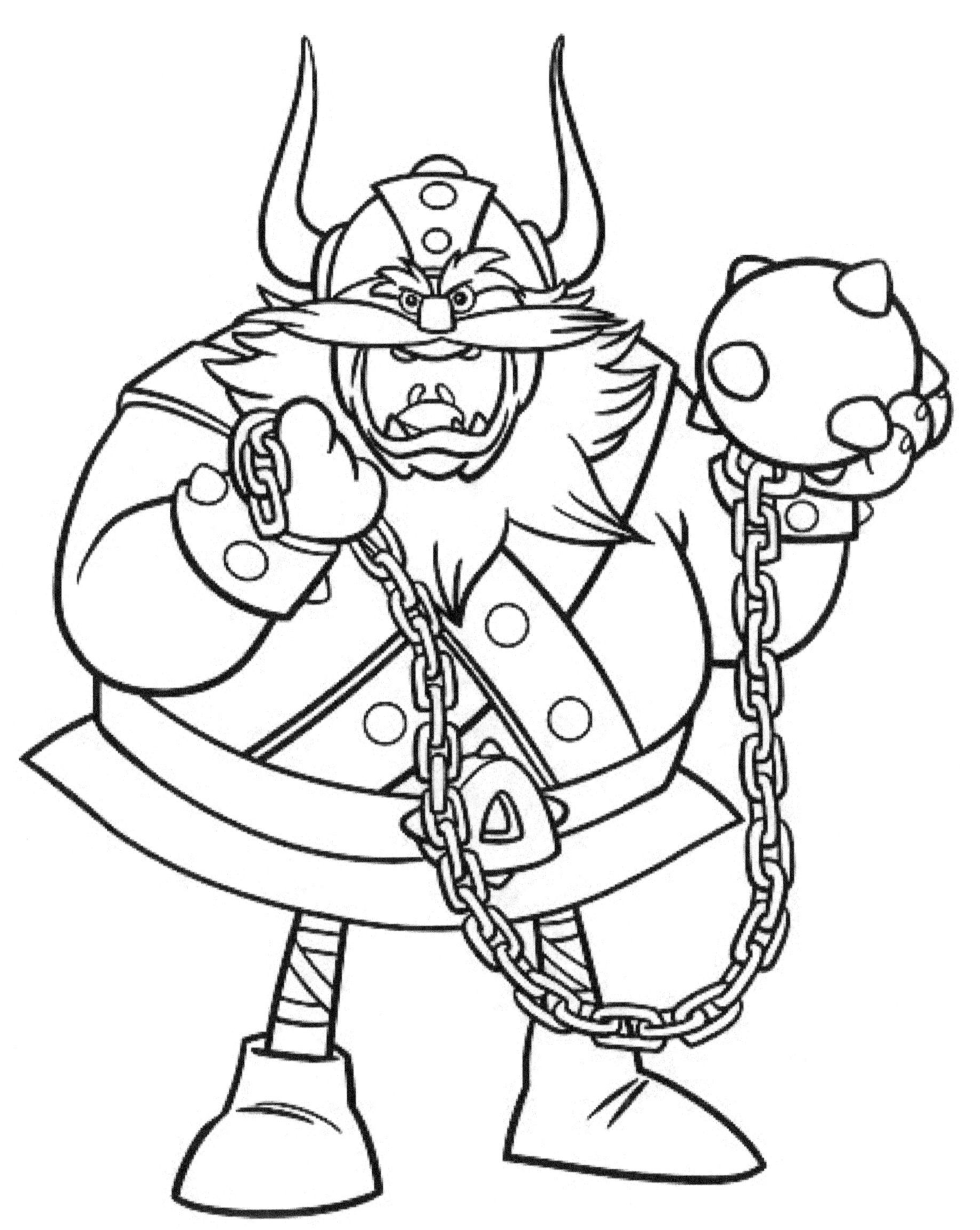

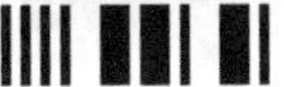

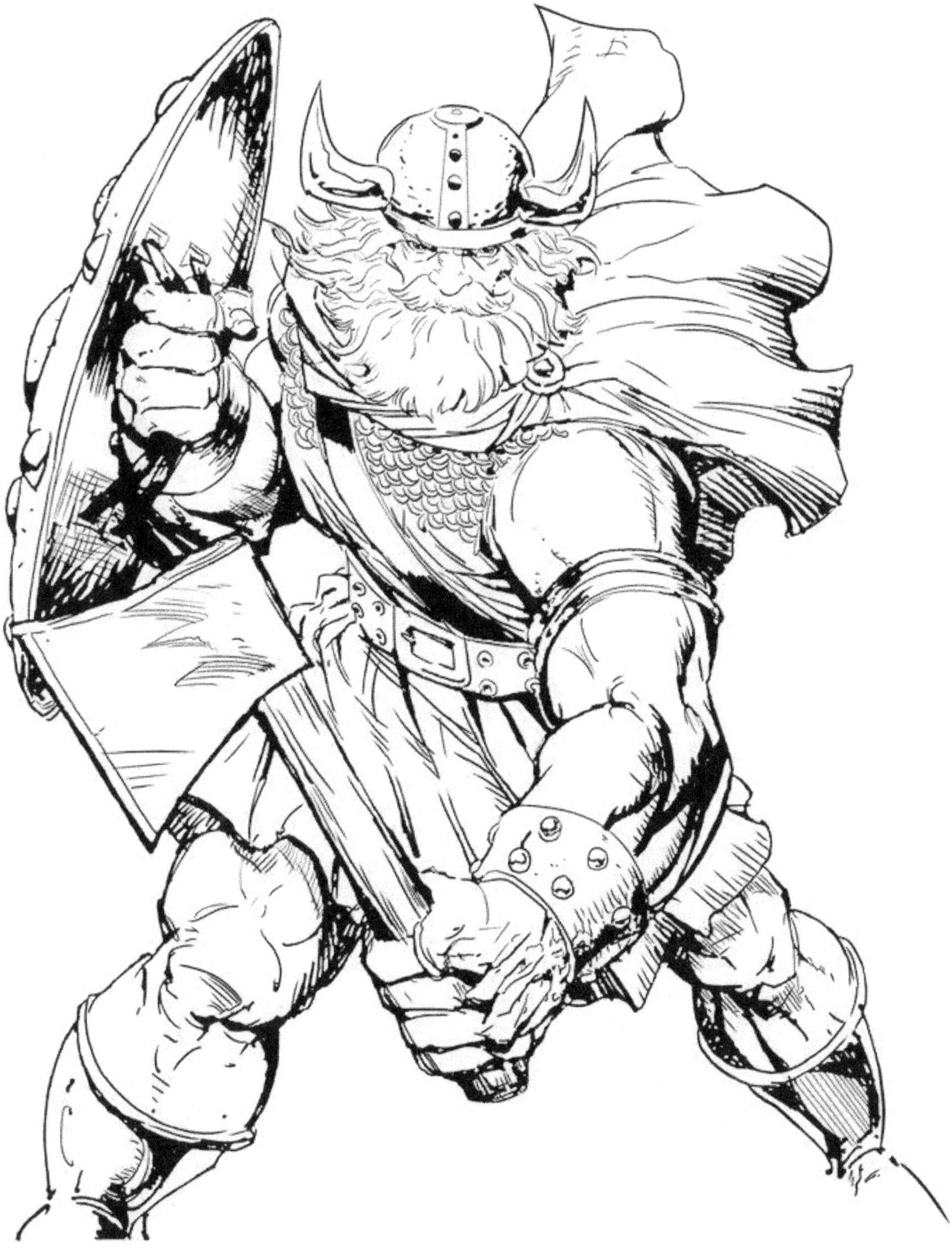

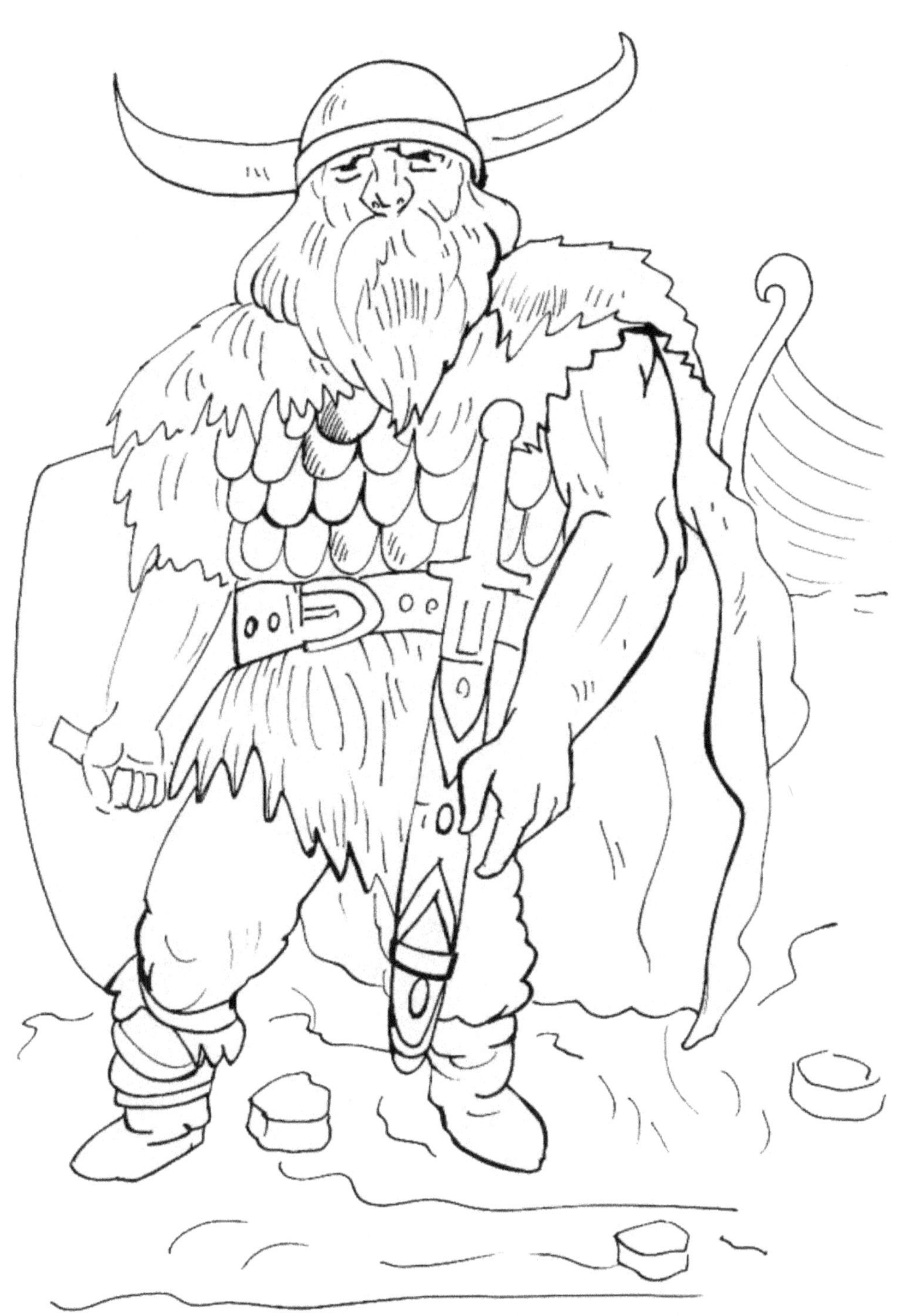

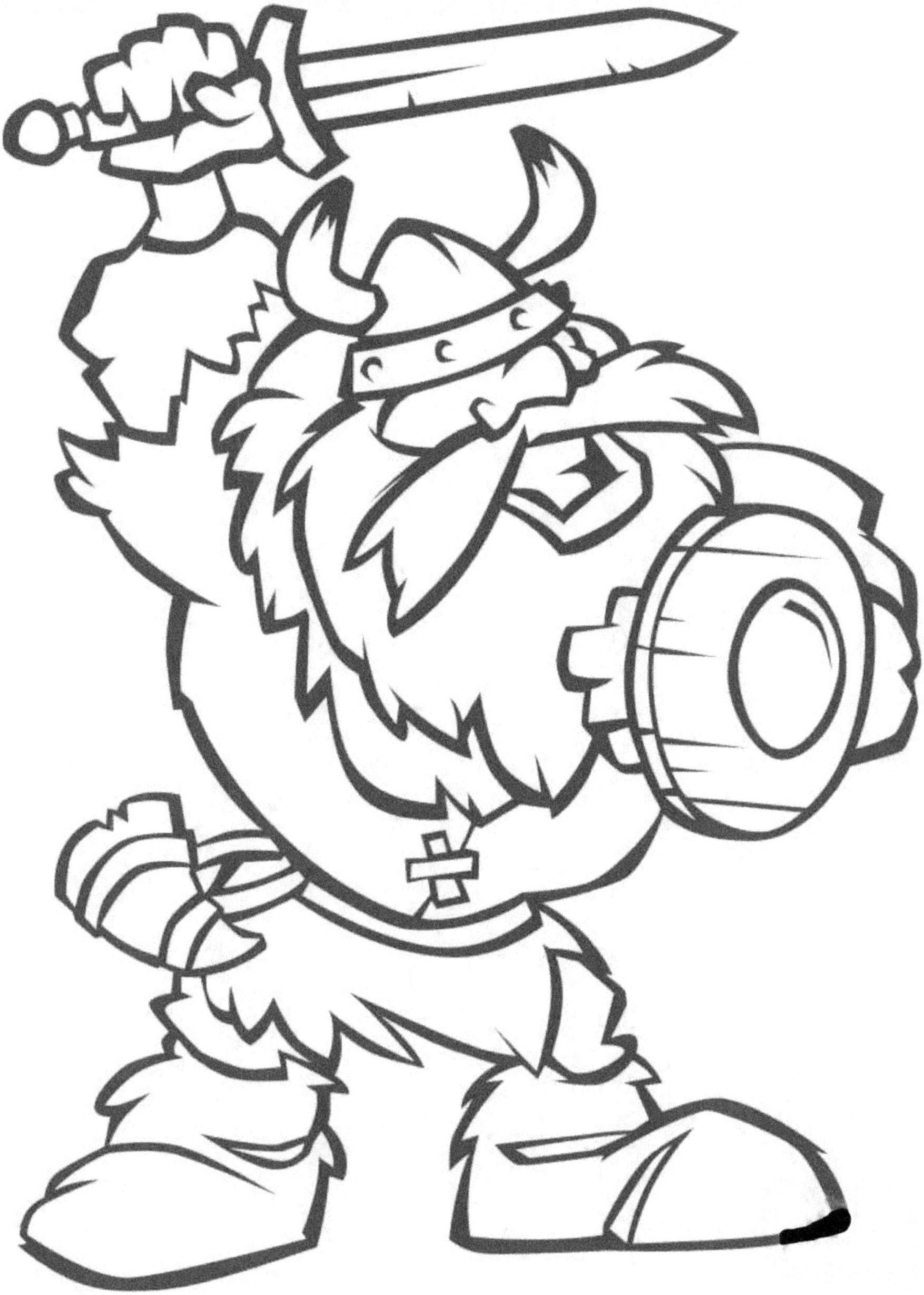

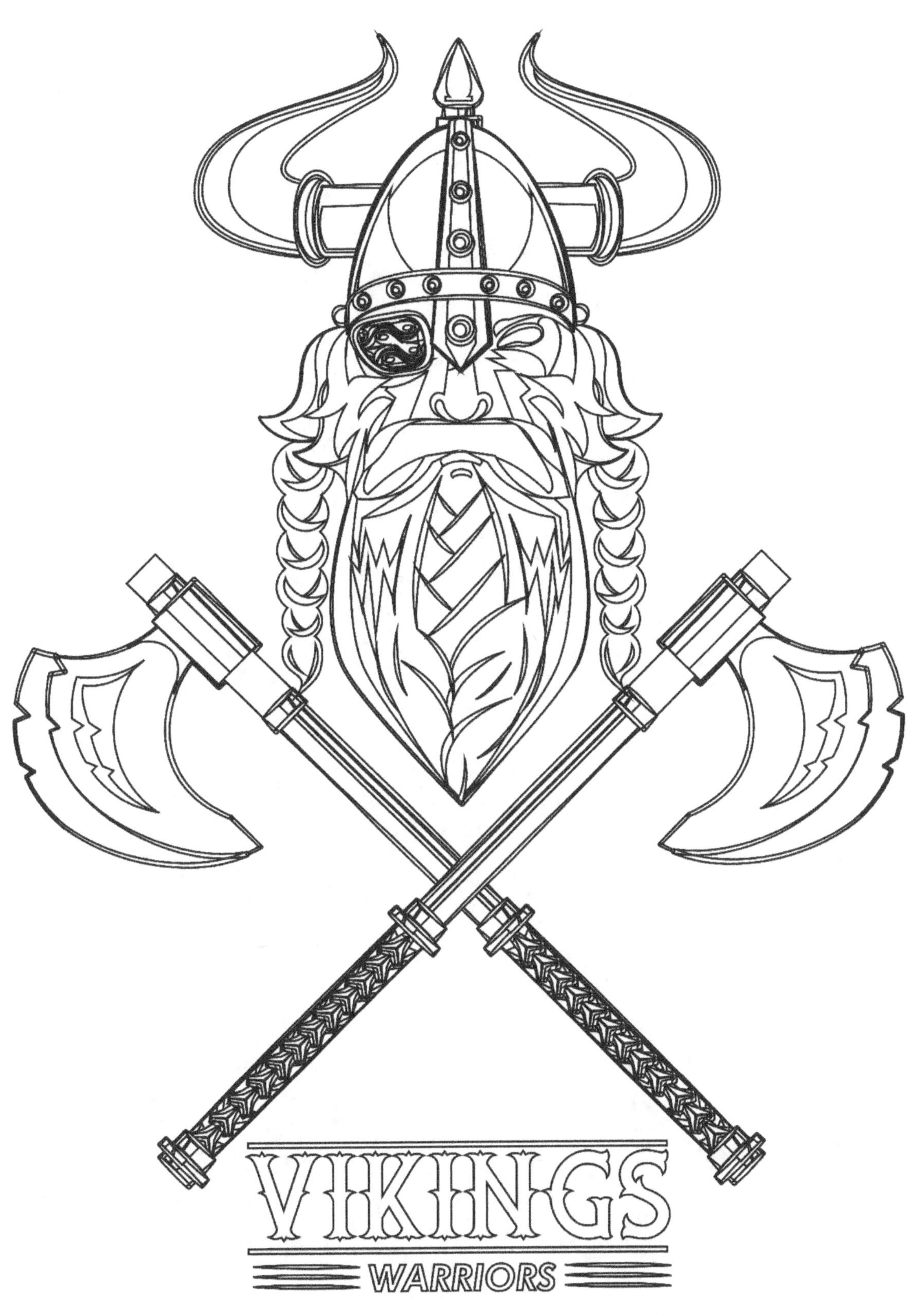

VIKINGS
WARRIORS

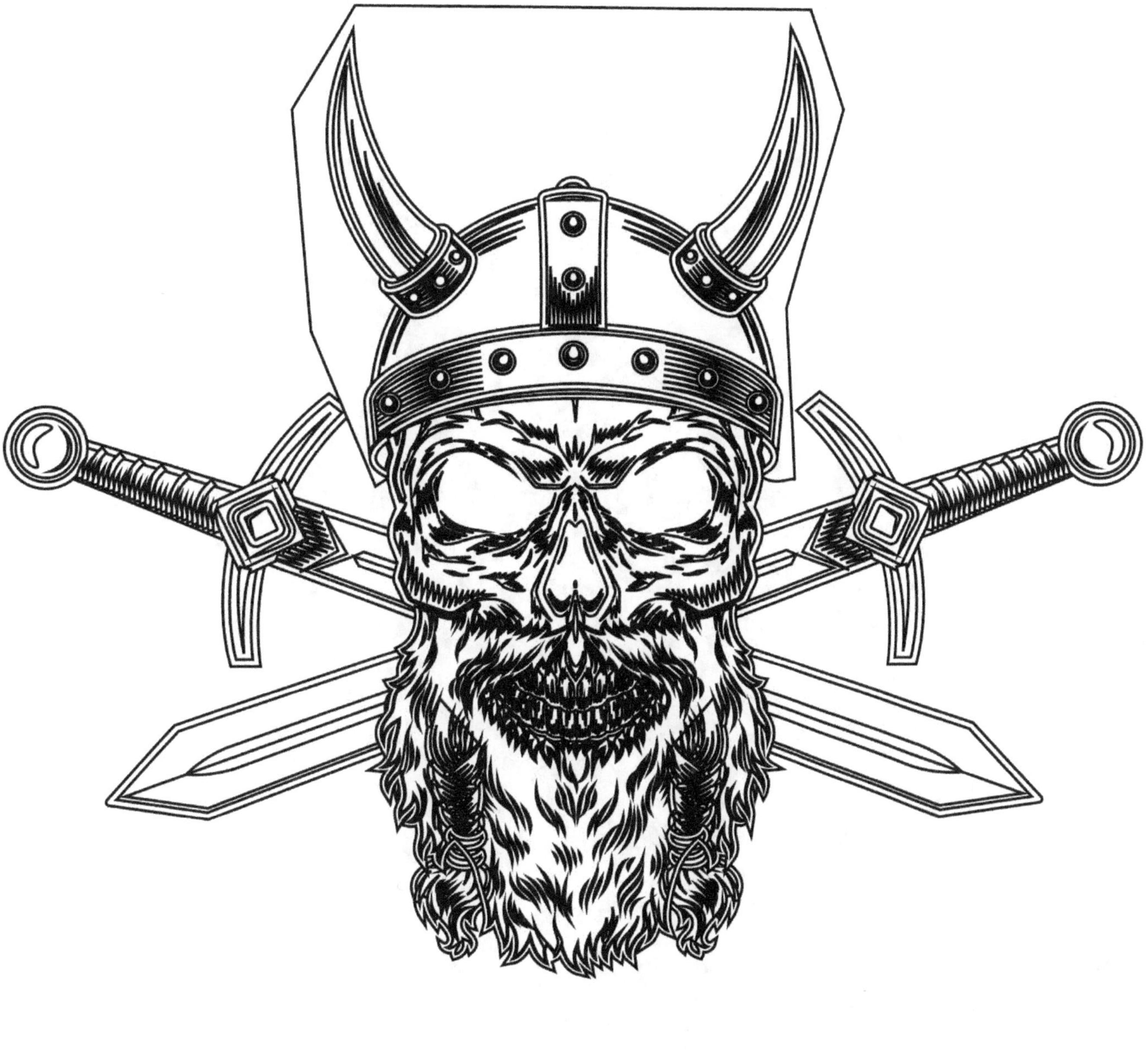

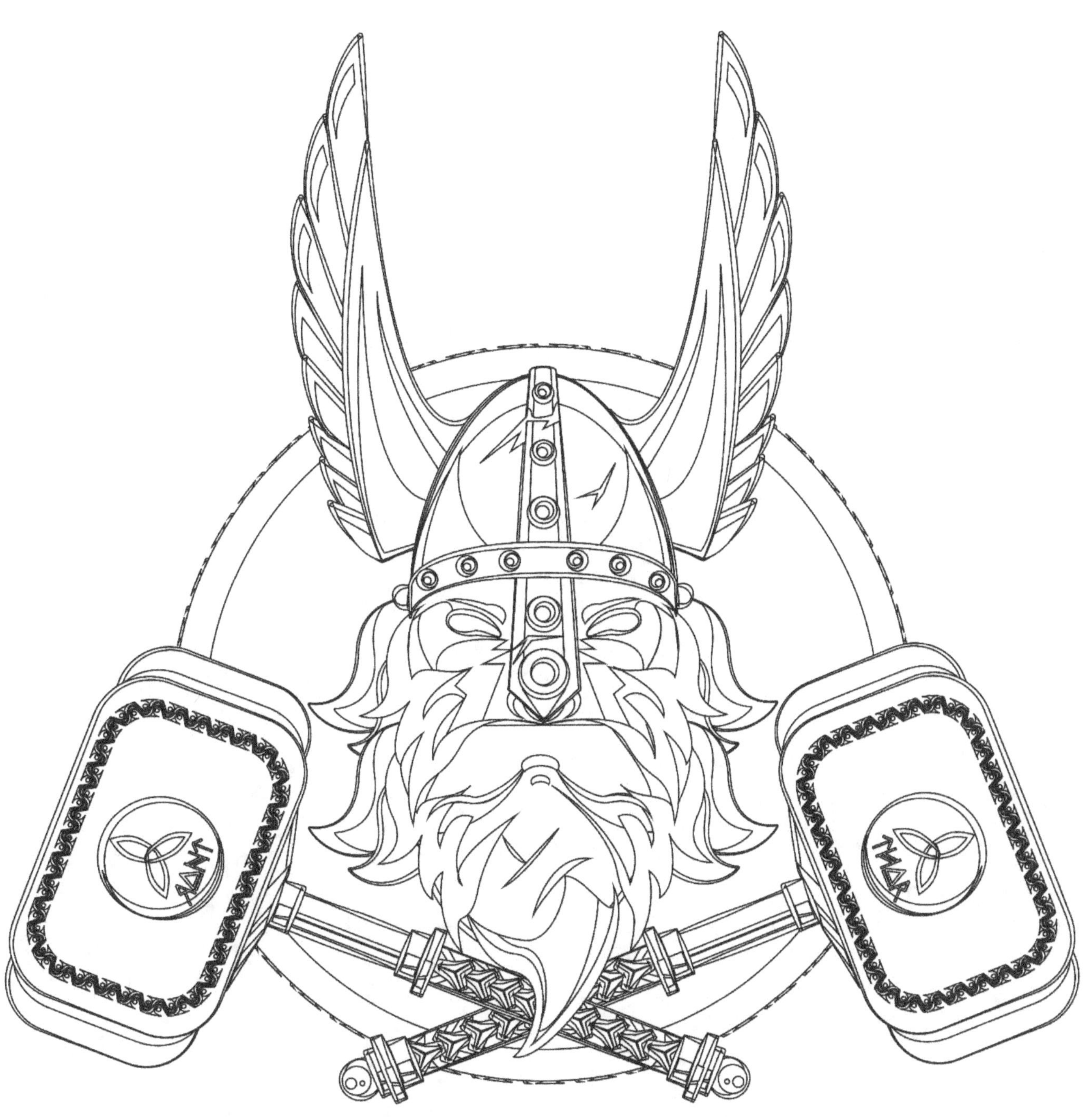

VIKINGS
THOR

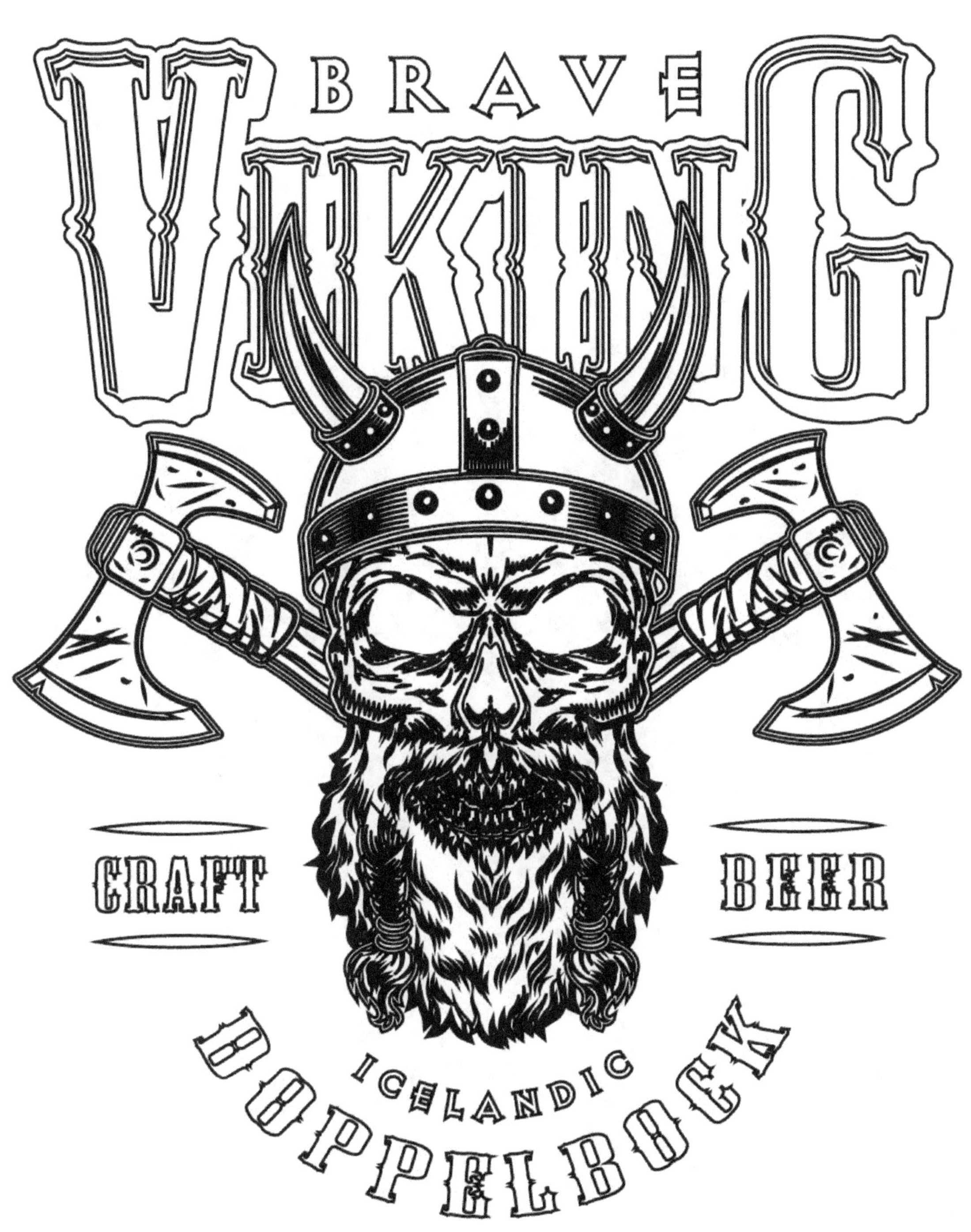

BRAVE
VIKING
CRAFT
BEER
ICELANDIC
DOPPELBOCK

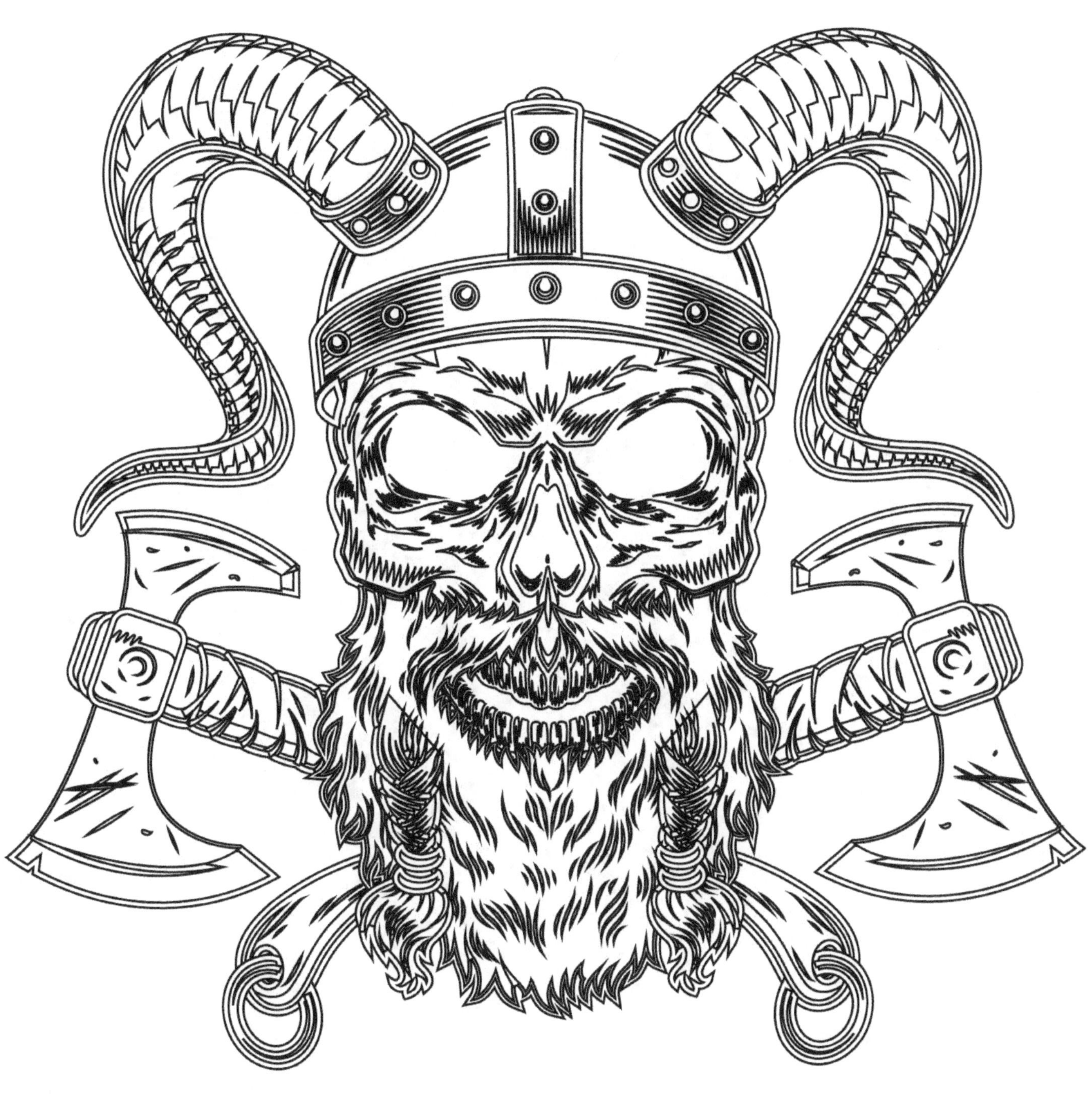

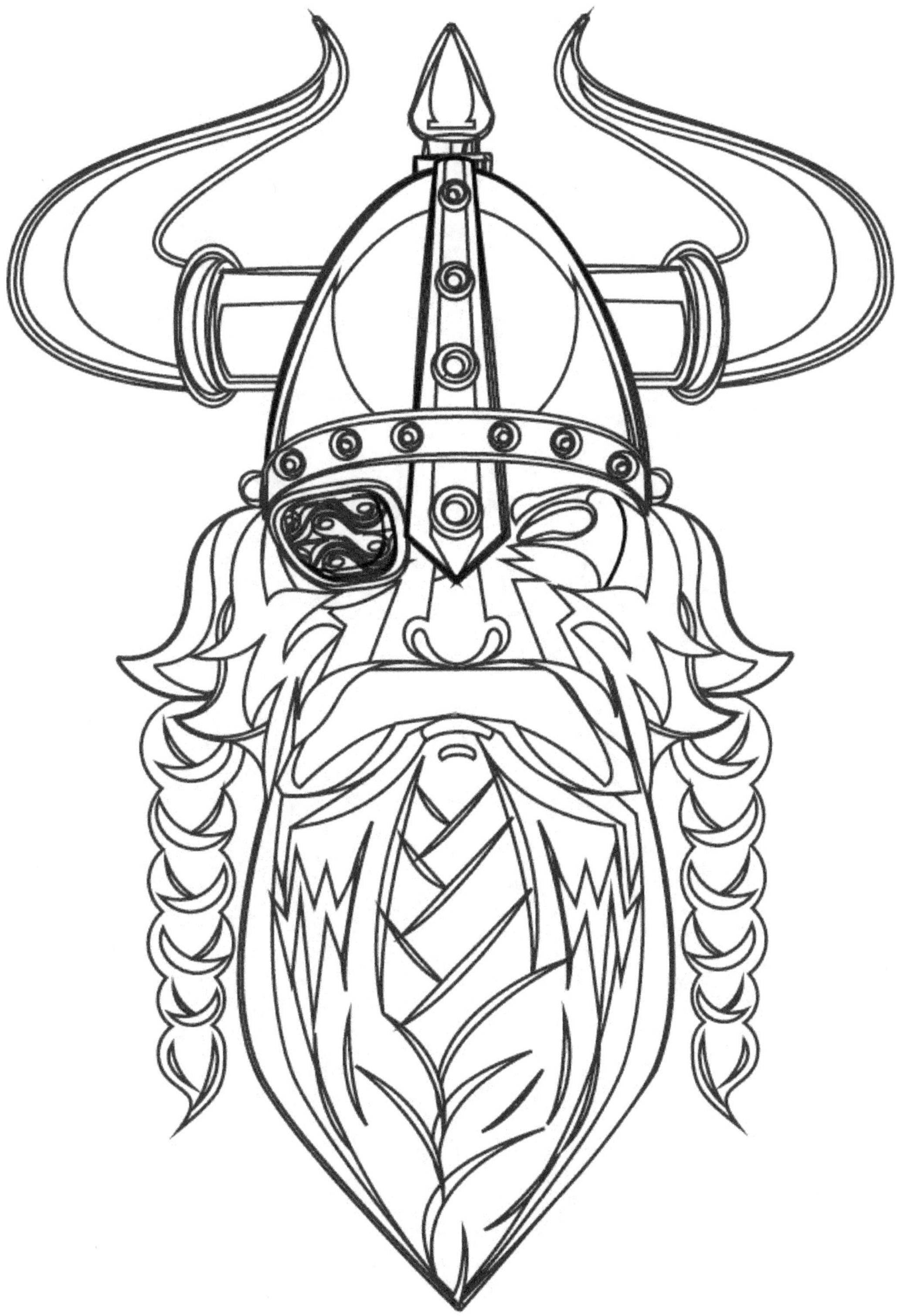

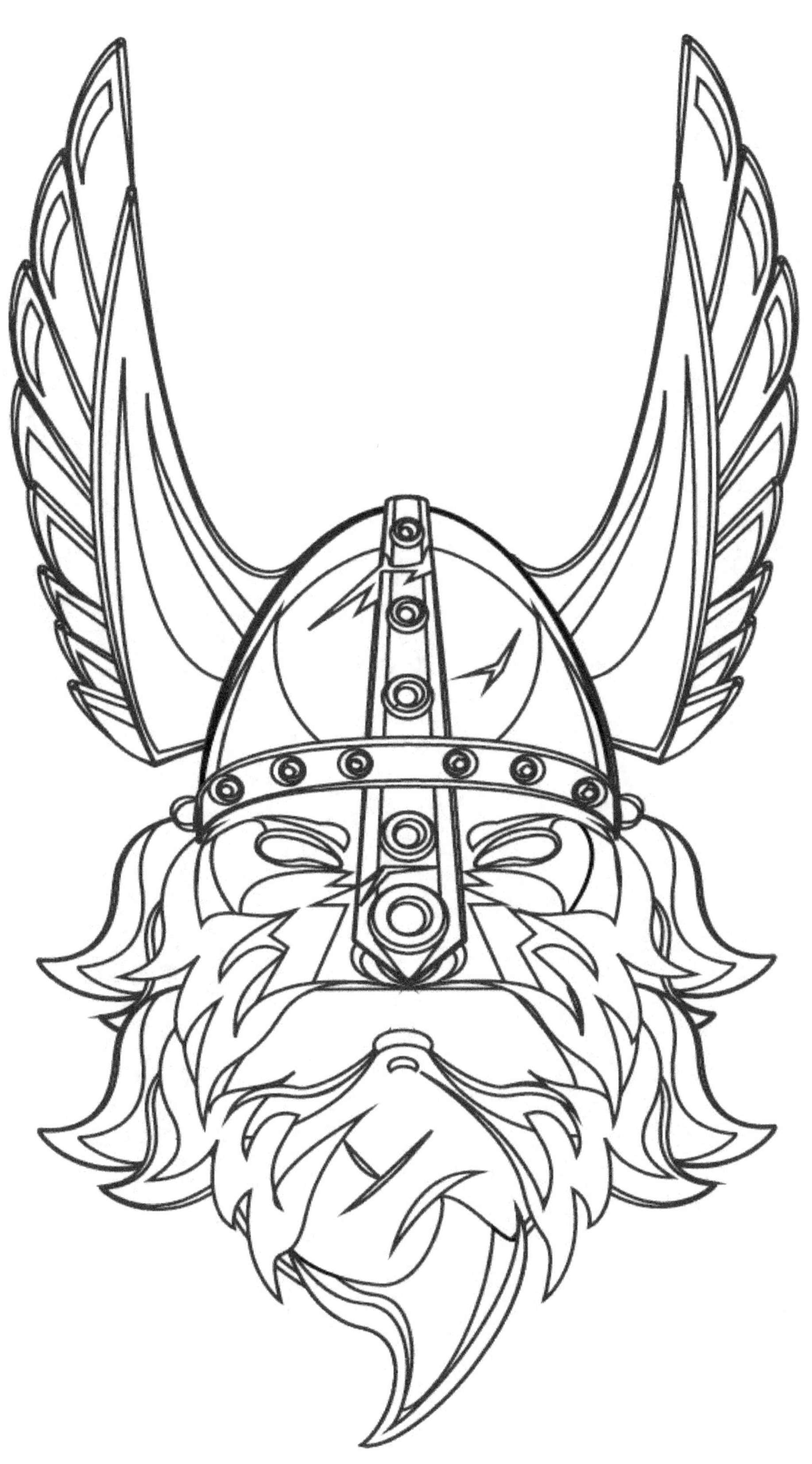

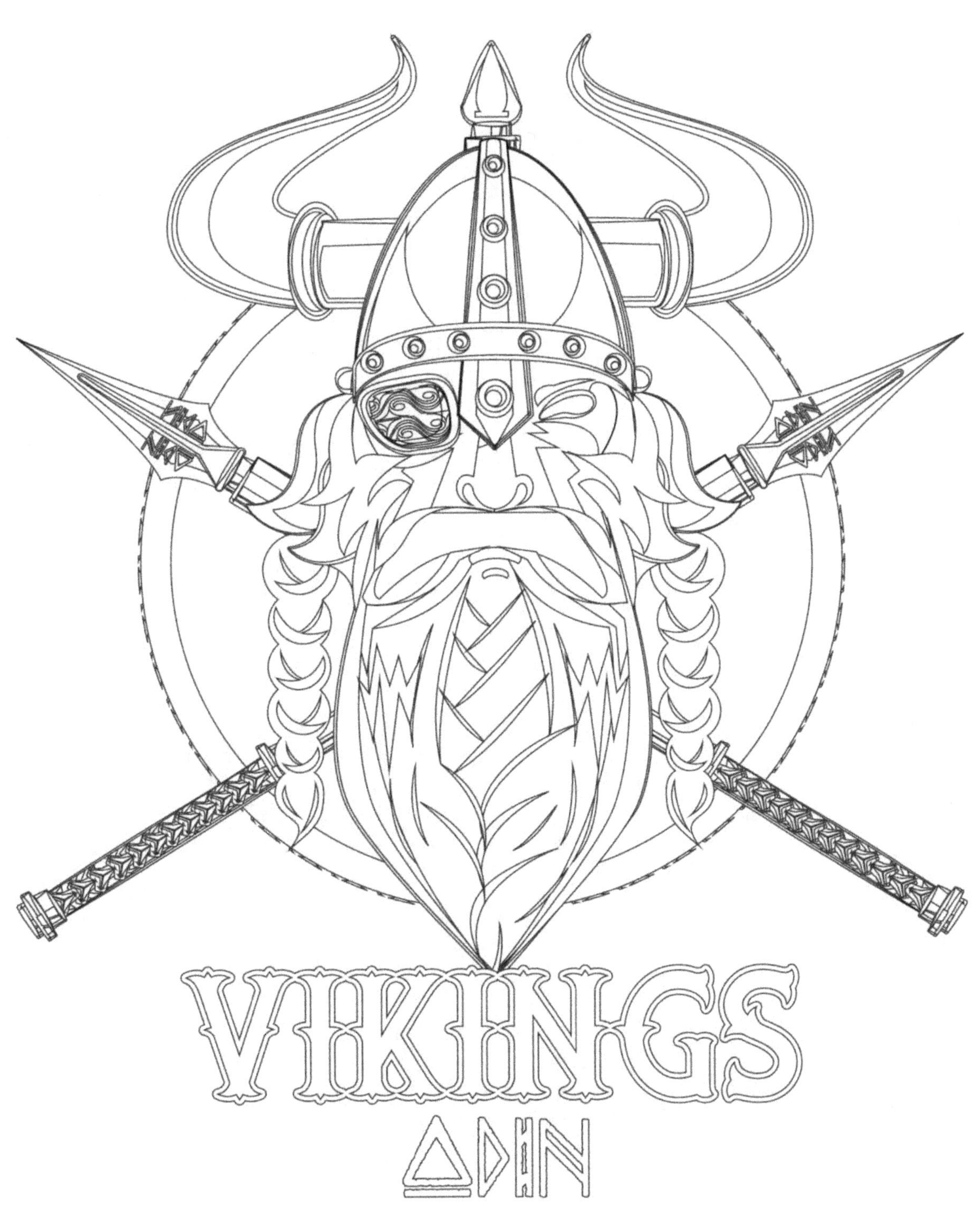

VIKINGS
ODIN